SCORNFLAKES

ATTILA THE STOCKBROKER

I was born John Baine in 1957 and grew up near Shoreham Harbour in Southwick, West Sussex, the only son of Muriel, a pianist, and Bill, a poet who left school at 14 and worked in the civil service for 46 years. My father's limited opportunities and enthusiasm for words, transmitted to me before he died in 1968, made me determined to get out there, say what I think and earn a living as a poet – something which all the critics tell you is impossible to do in this country. I've often wished I could tell you, Bill – I've managed it since 1982.

But this is not so much a living as a vocation; I really did begin this thing believing I – we – could help to make this world a happier and more equal place, and the fact that Newspeak is now reality, everything that my parents' generation fought for is being destroyed and the atmosphere in this country is getting more squalid, selfish and unpleasant by the minute just makes me angrier and more determined not to throw in the towel. For all those on the Left throughout the world whose eyes are dulled and spirit shattered by years of defeat I say: do not go gently. *Scornflakes* is for you.

ATTILA THE STOCKBROKER

SCORNFLAKES

illustrated by
WOMBLE

BLOODAXE BOOKS

ISBN: 1 85224 231 0

First published 1992 by
Bloodaxe Books Ltd,
P.O. Box 1SN,
Newcastle upon Tyne NE99 1SN.

Bloodaxe Books Ltd acknowledges
the financial assistance of Northern Arts.

Cover printing by J. Thomson Colour Printers Ltd, Glasgow.

Printed in Great Britain by
Bell & Bain Limited, Glasgow, Scotland.

For Joy

Acknowledgements

Poems in this collections have appeared in various anthologies including *Grandchildren of Albion, Hard Lines 2, Apples & Snakes 1* and *2, Prism* and many more, and in magazines, fanzines and other publications large and small all over the world. They've been read on radio and TV and performed in arts centres, rock venues, libraries, pubs, comedy clubs, colleges, folk clubs, schools, at open-air festivals, on trains and football terraces and in a hotel basement in Albania. 'Contributory Negligence', 'Vegetables' and 'Video Nazis' were first published in my 1985 collection *Cautionary Tales for Dead Commuters* (Unwin Paperbacks).

The illustrations were done by **Womble**, aka Dave T, who apart from being probably the world's only rock 'n' roll dentist is the publisher of an excellent magazine called *Wake Up*, combining hard-hitting political satire, excellently informative and well-researched articles, band interviews and loads more cartoons like the ones in this book! Issue 9 £2 inc p&p; issue 10 £3 inc p&p from Womble, P.O. Box 34, Oulton, Lowestoft, Suffolk NR33 9QG.

If you want to write to me you can do so c/o Bloodaxe Books, P.O. Box 1SN, Newcastle upon Tyne NE99 1SN. I promise you'll get a reply.

Contents

Publications by Attila the Stockbroker

BOOKS

Cautionary Tales for Dead Commuters (Unwin, 1985: out of print)
(ed.) *In Praise of Slough* (1988 – thankfully out of print!)
Scornflakes (Bloodaxe Books, 1992: alive and kicking)

LPs / CDs

Ranting at the Nation (1983: deleted)
Sawdust and Empire (1984: deleted)
Libyan Students from Hell! (1987: kaput)
Scornflakes (1988)
Live at the Rivoli (Canada, 1990)
Donkeys' Years (1991)
This Is Free Europe (𝔊𝔢𝔯𝔪𝔞𝔫𝔶, 1992)
668 – Neighbour of the Beast (Australia/New Zealand, 1992)
plus various singles & tracks on compilation albums

For further information on any of these releases
write to me c/o Bloodaxe.

Rage, rage against the dying of the light.

DYLAN THOMAS

Repossessed by the Devil

In the days of the old never-never
when your house rose in price with each day
in a right to buy giveaway con-trick
to make millions vote Margaret's way
you mortgaged your income to Satan
Doctor Faustus of Shoreham-by-Sea
saw the homeless in the bed & breakfasts
and thought how the hell can that be

So, you borrowed the earth in the eighties
when the plastic explosion held sway
Your repayments are late so this is your fate –
repossessed by the Devil today

Now you used to be prudent and thrifty
till Satan's slaves took you in hand
You are what you buy was the corporate cry
in a don't pay till next year land
No matter you're stretched to the limit
To our credit, we'll offer you more
But now all the chickens have come home to roost
There are men in grey minds at the door

You were top of the tree in the eighties
when the plastic explosion held sway
You bought crap on a whim now you're out on a limb –
repossessed by the Devil today

In the London hotels where the suits go to lunch
if you beg your way into the feast
you'll see Major, the Devil's trainspotter
and the Chancellor, the neighbour of the beast
making jokes with their friends in the City
whose promises put you in hock
and talking of regeneration
while the bailiffs are changing the lock

But again you believed what they told you
on your hand-picked excursion to Hell
'Ah, it's better the Devil you know, mate!'
Now you've got to know him far too well...

A man was beaten to death in August 1992 at a burger stall in
Kingston-upon-Thames apparently because, though English, he
was speaking in French to his female companions...

Language Barrier

'Oi, you!
Whaddya talking foreign for?
You're English like us, aintcha?
So whaddya talking foreign for?
Nice birds though, ya done alright there, mate
But watcha talking like that for?
Oh, they don't speak English, don't they?
Well, whyya bovvering with them Froggie slags then?
Talking never did any good anyway – give us 'em over 'ere, they can
        talk to our meat, that's Esperanto, innit?
Watcha sayin to em? Oi, cunt, watcha sayin to 'em?
Talkin bahrt us, are ya?
Fuckin wanker
Bet ya think yer really clever-clever, dontcha,
talking foreign so we can't understand ya
trying to impress those birds with yer fancy lingo –
fucking university wanker
Hey, Del boy, shall we TALK to 'im, eh?
Poncy cunt – let's teach him a REAL lesson, eh?
Oh, not so mouthy now, are we, wanker?
Well, it's too late – we're gonna kick some good British sense into
        yer, aren't we, lads?
No use begging now, ya student tosser!'

and the boots went in
the fists went in
and he went down
the boots went in again
the fists went in again
and the lights went out on a life
destroyed in a blind moment of hatred
by the psychopathic flotsam of Thatcherism's own –
and let's have no excuses,
no bullshit sociology,

no talk of deprivation, of mitigating circumstances –
Kingston-on-Thames?
No, these were just mean-spirited scum,
celebrating the values of the last thirteen years –
the values of crass ignorance
selfishness
violence
and of course
'pride in being British'.
Was it for this, the 1944 Education Act?

People are murdered every day, of course
- in this nasty, brutish zit of a country,
often for even more unbelievably banal reasons –
so why this poem?
Simply that I remember
a visit to a pub
my own bilingual conversation
(it's a skill, you know, you learn it, like medicine or carpentry –
a skill that most Europeans take for granted)
and the broken beer glass
and the contorted face of the thug
when I replied to his insult in his own tongue –
For me it ended differently
but when I saw that story in the paper
a shiver ran down my spine
I remembered that evening in the pub
and the impotent anger swelled uncontrollably in my guts...

One final thought;
I bet THIS senseless murder
didn't make the tabloid headlines:
After all,
The Paper That Supports Our Boys
wouldn't want to alienate its readership,
would it?

In the vanguard of the stultifying wave of social and political apathy currently festering across our nation we find The Kids. Their immediate forebears were radical hippies and wild-eyed punk rockers who rioted, vomited, went on demonstrations and generally stood up and spat. This bunch – who've actually got far more to be angry about than the last couple of generations – seem happier with a sensible haircut, a nice cup of cocoa and a Chris Rea LP.

The Blank Generation
(A new slant on an age-old theme)

The youth of today don't know they're born
...at the age of five, they're mowing the lawn

By the time they're eight, their golden dream
is a foolproof, high-yield pension scheme

As puberty strikes, know where they are?
Out there on Sundays, washing the car

Birthdays and Christmas, the same old cry:
'Please, please, Mum, can I have a new tie?'

Games: 'You be a company director,
I'll be the local tax inspector.'

Teenage rebellion: 'Grow up, Dad,
and buy a suit, you look real sad!'

Music: Doors and Rolling Stones (!)
and bleepy acid monotones*

(*though some are really daring creatures –
they like Blur and the Manic Street Preachers)

Politics: Grey. A tinge of green
from time to time, to suit the scene.

Ideals? 'Er…well…to earn a wage,
and quickly attain middle age.

Changing the world? For god's sake, no!
Our parents tried THAT years ago!'

*   *   *

I see no need to mince my words.
HEY, GET A LIFE, YOU BORING NERDS!

'Come friendly bombs, and fall on Slough
It isn't fit for humans now...'

Fifty years ago, in a moment of ill-informed spitefulness, the
Laureate and knighthood-destined John Betjeman cast a grievous
poetic slur on an innocent Berkshire town. Having lived in Har-
low for eleven years I have every sympathy with those who see
their most cherished locations subjected to cruel and unfounded
abuse – and so, on behalf of the newly-founded Slough Tourist
Board, incorporating the Berkshire Riviera Appreciation Society,
I thought it was time to redress the balance...

Slough

Come tourists all, and flock to Slough
as many as the streets allow
by car, or train – no matter how –
Come, very soon!

And lift forever the sad curse
once laid in dull, sarcastic verse
by one whose poetry is worse
than Mills and Boon!

Sir John – oh, what a sense of farce!
A poet of the teacup class
obsessed with railways, and stained glass
and twisted bough

and thus impervious to the call
of the post-war suburban sprawl
of Harlow, Basingstoke and all
and glorious Slough!

Oh Slough! Harbinger of my dreams!
Home of a thousand training schemes
and theme pubs, patronised by streams
of tetchy men

16

with blow-dried hair and blow-dulled brain
diplomas in inflicting pain
and ne'er a thought for Larkin, Raine
and Betjeman!

A thousand jewellers' shops contend
The kitchen unit is your friend
Designer labels set the trend
with a blank stare

And now – the latest, brightest star –
a brand new ten screen cinema!
The folk will come from near and far
to worship there!

Oh self-made, independent town!
The jewel in Albion's Southern crown!
No more will poets put you down
with mocking voice!

Come tourists all, and flock to Slough
as Milton Friedman takes a bow
This town is fit for heroes now –
Come, and rejoice!

And I am joined in my spirited defence of the Berkshire Riviera by some of our most estimable literary forebears! Yes, Bards throughout the ages have been moved to write in praise of Slough – and since many of them were treading this mortal coil before Slough was even a glint in the town planner's eye, one can only assume it was the *idea* of Slough which moved them to such fulsome praise…

'I must go down to Slough again
where the aeroplanes fill the sky
And all I ask is a Heathrow jet
with a whine like a drunken fly'
    JOHN MASEFIELD

'If I should die, think only this of me
That there's some corner of a foreign field
That is forever Slough'
    RUPERT BROOKE

'All things bright and beautiful
All creatures great and small
All things wise and wonderful
The Lord God made them Slough'
    CECIL ALEXANDER

'The curfew tolls the knell of parting day
The lowing herd winds slowly o'er the lea
The ploughman homeward plods his weary way
And I return to Slough to have my tea'
    THOMAS GRAY

'I can resist everything except Slough'
    OSCAR WILDE

'Now is the winter of our discontent
Made glorious Slough'
    WILLIAM SHAKESPEARE

Belgium

In the mountains of Belgium,
just outside Gent,
I take your arm
and, apprehensively,
we begin our descent.
On chariots of wire, we wander
the high walled peaks
of this consumer paradise
and I marvel
at the natural beauty
and fertility
of a Flemish valley.
Suddenly the checkout lady,
noticing my vacant stare,
enquires if I need the toilet,
curses in a guttural burp,
and throws us onto the street.
Mountaineering in Belgium
is not as simple
as it looks.

Worthing

On the beach at Worthing
the lugworm casts
by the sewage outfall
look like dirty shepherd's pie.
We walk the shingle
hand in hand
and the crabs
on the nearby groyne
remind me of more intimate times.
Your hand resembles a limp flounder.
I squeeze it dispassionately.
The seaweed smells like a dirty toilet.
Refreshed, we return for dinner.

9 April 1992
(the fourth term)

Harlow

There was a grey fellow called Jerry*
who made us all nauseous, very.
But in Roydon and Nazeing
his vote was amazing!
I hope he falls under a ferry

(then he really would be a herald of free enterprise)

Basildon

In a carefully executed manoeuvre
which had been planned for several years
and to the chagrin of those on the Left
who still had faith in her,
a proletarian chirpy cockney sacred cow
suffering from terminal BSE
(Brain Surgery by Editorial –
otherwise known as Mad Cower Disease)
was led, mooing contentedly,
into a polling booth
and from there
into an economic slaughterhouse;
stunned by a series of shocks from the Treasury
bled dry by the building societies
and thrown into the dustbin of history
she still could be heard lowing pathetically
'it'd be worse under Labour…
it'd be worse under Labour…'

*Jerry Hayes, MP (sadly)

Recently that friend of intelligent journalism and editorial freedom, Rupert Murdoch, took over William Collins – a publishing house which, among other things, produces the Bible. I can now reveal the planned New Revised Version...

The Bible according to Rupert Murdoch

In the beginning was the Word, and the Word was Gotcha! And the Lord Rupert said let there be a Royal Family, and let enormous quantities of trivia and drivel be written about them, yea even unto the point where a mentally subnormal yak couldn't possibly find it interesting any more, and let babies be born unto this Royal Family, and let the huge swathes of nauseating sludge written about them surpass even that written about their parents, even though these babies and their parents are about as interesting as a wet afternoon on the terraces at Selhurst Park.

And the Lord Rupert said let there be soap operas, and let each of these soap operas be so mind-numbingly moronic as to make a wet afternoon at Selhurst Park seem a truly uplifting experience, and let entire forests and the ecological balance of several continents be destroyed in the endless vistas of retarded outpourings about these unspeakable transmissions.

And let there be enormous breasts, and endless bonking, and hours and days and weeks and months and years of chauvinistic right-wing propaganda so that the brain-dead prats who like the bonking and the soap operas and the breasts and the royal stories get the politics as well.

And let any journalist who tries to stand up to the proprietor and editor in the name of truth, and intelligence, and integrity, and journalistic standards, be summarily dismissed, and cast forever into a bottomless pit of decomposing chimpanzee smegma, and let those journalists who suffer this fate rejoice at the great career move they have just made.

And the Lord Rupert looked at his work, and even he saw that it was a load of crap, but this was the enterprise culture and it sold millions so it was good. And on the same basis he decided to take over the television too, and the earth itself wept, and little robins vomited, and cuddly furry animals threw themselves under trains, and the whole thing was filmed by Sky Channel for a horror nature programme, and the most awful thing of all was that this was just the beginning...

A poem I wrote ten years ago, but which is, sadly, just as relevant today. A High Court Judge called Judge Richards said that a woman who was hitch-hiking late at night and was picked up and raped was 'asking for it' and guilty of contributory negligence...

Contributory Negligence

Hitching up the M11
coming back from an Upstarts gig
got picked up 'bout half eleven
by this bloke in a funny wig...
Flash Mercedes, new and gleaming
deep pile suits and deep seat piles
I got in and sat there scheming
while the dickhead flashed me smiles

Told me he was back from sessions
with a load of brain-dead hacks
Told me he'd made no concessions
to the bootboys and the blacks
Said he thought that it was stupid
fuss 'bout rapists on the news
Bloke was only playing Cupid
Girls like that they don't refuse

Asked me if I thought him enemy
Asked me if I bore a grudge
Told me that he came from Henley
Said he was a High Court judge
I asked him to stop a second
'Need a slash' that's what I said
When he did the anger beckoned
and I smacked him in the head

Took his keys and took his money
Crashed the car into a ditch
Though he moaned 'they'll get you, sonny!'
got away without a hitch
I don't think they'll ever find me
'cos I'm many miles away
but if one day they're right behind me
I know what I'm gonna say –

HE ASKED FOR IT! He's rich and snobbish
right wing, racist, sexist too
Brain-dead, ugly, sick and slobbish
Should be locked in London Zoo!
He wanted me to beat him up –
it was an open invitation!
Late at night he picked me up –
an act of open provocation!

High Court Judges are a blight –
they should stay home in nice warm beds
and if they must drive late at night
should never pick up Harlow Reds!
A five pence fine is right and proper
and to sum up my defence
It was his fault he came a cropper –
CONTRIBUTORY NEGLIGENCE!

THE WHITE HOUSE
WASHINGTON D.C.

Spring 1991

Dear Saddam (or can I call you Kevin?)

Well, it's all going wonderfully according to plan – the arms dealers are absolutely over the moon, the best sales demonstration in history, and we'll split the commission 50-50 as arranged – just don't tell that funny little Major guy or he'll want some, and that'd well and truly scupper our Harrods takeover bid, which'd be a real pity. Major's loving every minute of it – he thinks war's even more exciting than Trivial Pursuit and doing the washing up, and just as we planned they've forgotten all about his poll tax fiasco, our balance of payments deficit and your little Kurdish and Shi'ite problem...

Oh, by the way, that nice German pesticide firm wanted me to tell you that they've found a new gas formula which works even better than the old one; and Mitterrand says that even if I have to rearrange your air force in the next couple of weeks there are plenty more planes where those came from. Don't worry, feller, I've made sure that it's business as usual. There's going to have to be a bit of a turkey shoot, as we agreed – the folks back home are gagging for it – but I'm sure you've done as requested and conscripted all the political prisoners and Islamic militants into the front line so we can both kill two birds with one stone, as it were. God knows you don't want them taking the place over any more than I do.

And that brings me on to the bit I know you're worried about. Of course, we in the Pentagon are absolutely determined to keep you safely at the helm, don't worry – we never forget our old friends, and your continued presence is essential to maintain the balance of forces with those fundamentalist nutters, as you know. But just in case, we've got the escape route all worked out. We've found you and your lady wife a lovely little place in Guatemala City, right next to some of your favourite Nazi war criminals; Imelda Marcos does a lovely Chow Mein and you'll find Noriega and those Contra death squad chiefs great, er, shooting partners. I'm pretty confident that after the turkey shoot and a few bellicose swaggerings from yours truly the whole thing will blow over and we can come the good guys with the non-interference in the internal affairs bit, leaving you sitting pretty.

But don't worry – if the worst comes to the worst and we get rumbled, the exit is sorted. And you'll be back in the 'hot seat' in any case by mid-1992, 'cos as you know, you're my trump card in the election – forget that idiot Quayle, you're my real running mate, Saddy boy! Just make the right noises, put on the tin hat and make sure those military installations of yours are knee-deep in our least favourite sort of political prisoners – I'll do the rest. Maggie in '82, George in '92! It's amazing how the scent of blood gets 'em going, isn't it? Amazing, when I think about it, how the Republican Party delegates – the 'Party of the Family' – will be absolutely desperate for me to bomb a few Iraqi families to get myself elected again! Oh, well, that's war, I suppose. Isn't it wonderful?

Take care and get your handicap down – we'll be back on the links soon!

Yours,

Bushy

In 1985 the Americans bombed innocent women and children in Tripoli, using the Libyans as scapegoats for their own frustrations and blaming them, without any proof, for a series of attacks on American bases. I thought; why not take their attitude to its logical conclusion, and blame Libya for everything that has gone wrong throughout the whole of history? Since then the 'Russian Threat' (featured extensively in some of my earliest poems) has evaporated and it looks increasingly as though Arabs and Asians are going to be the West's new scapegoats (though we'll still sell them arms and side with them when it suits us, of course, won't we, Saddam?)

Libyan Students from Hell!
(a traditional Middle Eastern thrash metal song)

Just look at us – we're the scourge of the land
We're Colonel Gadaffi's favourite band
We all eat babies and we're Commies too
and we've all got AIDS and we'll give it to you
With scaly tails and horns and hooves
We undermine everything that moves
And we don't care just what you say
'cos you sold us the weapons anyway
So don't mess with us, cos we're foreign and we smell –
We're the Libyan Students from Hell!

If your telly goes wrong or your car won't start
You can bet your life that we played our part
If your team doesn't win or you miss the bus
Then ten to one it's all down to us
If a dog runs off with your copy of *The Sun*
and brings it back with the crossword done
If someone smacks you in the head
Or you find Jeffrey Archer in your bed
We did it – and everything else as well
'Cos we're Libyan Students from Hell!

There's nothing very prudent
about a Libyan student
Can't you tell?
There's nothing very prudent about a Libyan student
From Hell!

We imported *Neighbours* to these shores
We personally started both World Wars
We broke your Gran's Coronation mugs
We sold Ben Johnson all his drugs
We caused the Plague and the Great Fire too
And we brought *The Price Is Right* to you
We pushed Robert Maxwell over the side
And we took Marc Bolan for his last ride
And if you paid your Poll Tax – well
You're all LIBYAN STUDENTS FROM HELL!

A Sad Fate indeed is suffered by those who forsake the glorious path of Creativity and Stage Performance for the parasitic monstrosities of a career in Criticism. One such is a Friend of mine, whose Surname shall be withheld in order to spare him Further Shame...

A Cautionary Tale
Being the story of Steven, an Apprentice Poet who became a Music Journalist, and was sadly cut off in his Prime.

Young Steven was a Clever Thing
He used to Play, and Dance, and Sing
and cut up Worms, and smash up Chairs
and push Old Ladies down the Stairs
And as he grew, he got so Bold
he'd never do as he was told
and Ma and Pa got rather riled
about their sordid little Child...
But, following his Teenage Years,
and Spots, and all the Normal Fears,
Young Steven formed a Clever Plan
to make himself a Famous Man!
He tried the Stage, but sad to say
the Crowds told him to go away
so he – a normal recourse, this –
became a Music Journalist.
Before too long young Steven's Fame
was such, that mention of his Name
would bring Huge Gasps of Admiration
from Every Corner of the Nation!
His Articles (this made him proud)
were often Praised, and Read out Loud
as Prime Examples of the Art
of Careful Writing From The Heart.
His work won Prizes, and Awards
and Boat Trips on the Norfolk Broads
and soon young Steven was the toast
of Decent Folk from Coast to Coast...
But with this Adulation came
– a consequence of Wealth, and Fame –

the bold attentions of a Crowd
of Wicked Persons, Wild and Loud!
These Persons of Appalling Taste
made after Steve in Fearful Haste
and pinned Our Hero to the Floor
then had their Way, Twelve Hours or more...
And then some Sheep, some Rats and Mice
– and Other Creatures not so nice –
made Lustful Concourse with our Steve
and did things no one would believe
Things, sad to say, he did enjoy –
the Nasty and Perverted Boy.

Next morning, Steven woke in pain
and yelled for help – but all in vain
Then he gazed down in Shocked Surprise
at the Sad Sight that met his eyes...
A Sore large as a Human Ear
on Steven's Member did appear
and, sad to say, it grew and grew
(as Sores so very often do)
The Doctor came, and shook his Head
and filled Our Hero's Heart with Dread
a portent of an Awful Fate –
'Yes, we will have to amputate'
Now Steven's Pride and Joy is gone;
he sadly walks the Streets alone
with but a Stump, inflamed and gory...
here I shall end his Tragic Story.
The Moral of this Tale is clear;
If Young and Male, go drink some Beer
Write Poetry, have a furtive Wank
Hold Pickets outside Barclays Bank
Buy Morrissey LPs, wear Glasses
Do Good Things for the Working Classes
go Train Spotting, or take up Chess –
but don't write for the Music Press!

The Gulag Archipelago-go

Canvey Island Zen Stalinist Theme Gulag
12 June 2018

Dear Darren,

Been here nearly three months now, ever since the United Communist bastards stopped my car at the Hertfordshire border checkpoint and found that old Madonna tape and the copies of the *Underground Sun* I was trying to smuggle through. I reckon I'd have made it if it wasn't for that bastard sunstrip – no one told me they had been made illegal under that poxy new Articulacy Act and I hadn't bothered to take it off, which was a dead giveaway. I was shitting myself when I got here, what with all the rumours about those Red bastards torturing people with books and chess sets and copies of the *Guardian* and so on, but, believe it or not, I'm having a great time! Yeah, straight up!

Didn't look good to begin with though. When they checked us through the perimeter gates things were really grim. The whole of the camp is surrounded by this huge moat full of what looks like soya milk, and it's guarded by loads of pit bull terriers with really fierce lesbians on long leads – even if you get through them, there are two huge barbed wire perimeter fences that really rip your clothes, with an illuminated strip in the middle covered in that really thick motor oil that absolutely ruins your trainers. Anyone who did manage to get out would be looking at well over a grand for a completely new set of gear, at least. And the illuminated oil strip is kept under constant surveillance by hundreds of teachers and social workers who watch your every movement from massive ivory towers. It was well scary, I can tell you!

But when we got inside…wow! First of all, we were met by these really nice birds who gave us all 'Canvey Island Zen Stalinist Theme Gulag' baseball caps, and then the camp commander – an old geezer called Billy something who seems alright, as it goes – gave us a welcoming speech in which he told us not to worry, the external security system was not at all representative of life inside, and as long as we didn't try to escape we'd all have a whale of a time since the theme of this particular gulag was Saturday Night in August on the Costa del Sol, 24 hours a day, 365 days a year! And then the welcoming party started…

At first we couldn't believe it at all. After all, this was supposed to be the Reds' most notorious prison camp, the one no one had ever escaped from – but when they turned on the lager fountain and brought out the paella and the disco began I thought hey, why would anyone WANT to escape? If you lot in the Tory Resistance knew what was going on here you'd tear up your membership cards and start fighting the pit bulls and lesbians to try and get IN!

It's officially called a work camp, but there's hardly any work to do 'cos everything we need is flown in from your side – volunteers go down to the airstrip once a week to unload the food and videos and lager off the supply planes, and yours truly always volunteers of course, 'cos it means I get to "lose" some of the stuff on the way back, if you get my drift, though there isn't much point actually since everything's free anyway. Old habits die hard, eh? But the rest of the time – party! Unlimited free condoms! Unlimited booze! We've got cable TV with 215 channels, and we've even got our own camp newspaper, run by the bloke who owned that *Sunday Sport* before the revolution – so you guessed it. PHWOAR! None of that boring news stuff at all! Though I hear rumours that things are pretty bad outside – apparently the Reds have renationalised the air industry now. Bloody Commie bastards! You know what we used to say in the good old days – there's no such thing as a free breath!

All in all, what with their bloody Articulacy Act and the raising of the school leaving age to 20 and all that socialism and nationalisation and health service nonsense (whoever thought we'd be hearing that rubbish again, I thought the 1990s killed it off for good!) I reckon I'm better off in here!

Although I must tell you that there's one thing here that really worries me. Some of the people here, most of them actually, believe it or not, started to get bored with all the non-stop partying and discos and booze and sex and videos after a couple of months and they're going quite voluntarily into this big building marked REHABILITATION where all they do is sit around reading books and talking! Every day loads of teachers and social workers come down from their ivory towers on the camp boundary to take part in discussion groups and sometimes people don't come out of there for days – there's plenty of sleeping accommodation, and it's tucked away in a corner of the camp, and they just stay there!

And when they do come out...well, I can tell you, sometimes it's horrible. One of my best mates from the Resistance, an old fat bearded bloke who used to be quite a famous *Sun* journalist before the Reds rounded them up after the Battle of Wapping and stuck them in here, spent two whole weeks in rehabilitation and when he came out he started talking about Zen Stalinism and the United Communists' education programme and the bloody Articulacy Act and – get this – how the global AIDS plague wasn't the homosexuals' fault at all! He called me a neanderthal – I had to ask one of the teachers to tell me what it meant – and he even tried to get me to go to rehabilitation! I mean, what a traitor! I was going to get a few of the old gang together (though most of them are in rehabilitation too now, I'm sad to say) and give him a right old kicking, but the next thing I knew – he'd gone! 'I've gone over to the other side', the note read, 'to help supervise the returning of the United Kingdom's air supply to its proper place in the public domain!' Wanker!

Wey-hey! I've just seen the latest issue of the *Gulag Grope*, our paper! Talk about jugs! And I've got to go 'cos the curries are here, and there's another party starting in a couple of minutes. PARTYYYYY!! Hope you manage to destroy those new hospitals and schools the Reds are building – SMASH THE ARTICULACY ACT and GOD SAVE THE KING!! My so-called mates might be going soft but me – never! I reckon I might just pop down to rehabilitation tomorrow, though; just to check out the birds, like, not cos Zen Stalinism means anything to me, no way...

Rule Britannia!

Yours,
BARRY

Vegetables

No agony, no ecstasy, no pleasure and no pain –
so exquisitely uninteresting you drive your wife insane
The TV is your oracle, the newspapers your guide
and your shiny little vehicle is your passion and your pride
You've done the same things every day for nigh on forty years
and in your ludicrous routines you hide your worthless fears
On the blandest boat in Boredom you are captain of the crew –
and every time I eat vegetables it makes me think of you...

You died the day that you were born, and now you sit and rot
an empty-headed dinosaur in the pond that time forgot
Your image is respectable, there's nothing underneath
and the whole thing is as surely false as nine-tenths of your teeth
Your views are carbon copies of the rubbish that you read
and you swallow every morsel Rupert Murdoch seeks to feed
You go to bed at ten because you've nothing else to do –
and every time I eat vegetables it makes me think of you.

Your sex life is a catalogue of your poor wife's frustrations –
like thousands of Red Indians, she has her reservations
And so she took a lover; of course, you'll never know –
the last time you made love to her was many years ago
And if you had some spirit then it wouldn't be so bad:
it's your awesome anonymity which makes me get so mad
Your brain stem is a nether world where bored trainspotters queue
and every time I eat vegetables it makes me think of you.

You're a cabbage in a pickle and your brain has sprung a leek
so lettuce keep our distance 'cos I vomit when you speak
I'll always do a runner so I'm going where you've bean
'cos to see you chills my marrow and turns my tomatoes green
You're an eighteen carrot cretin with a dandelion whine –
so stick to your herbaceous border and I'll stick to mine
And although this verse is corny, it's amaizing but it's true
that every time I eat vegetables it makes me think of you!

To Slough and Sanity
(a Post-Martian Pastorale)

Far from our city haunts,
besieged on all sides,
we stumble apprehensively
through a minefield of cowpats.
The cloying earth
sucks greedily at your high heels
and you surrender reluctantly
to the ditch's embrace.
Crouching to your aid, I suddenly see before me
all of Flanders in 1916 –
trench, barbed wire, stinging nettles,
broken glass, maggots...
the stench of death!
As my outstretched arm levers you upright
you suggest that I may be guilty of pretentiousness
and ill-timed remarks...
and as I purse my lips in reply
the enemy come over the top!
Huge, lumbering tanks
lowing deeply:
an armoury of udders –
bitter mammaries indeed!
With a yell, I sound the alarm
and we beat a disorderly retreat
to Slough, and sanity.

Canada

I am playing at a plush, antiseptic businessman's dinner and dance establishment called the Norwood Hotel; it's my first gig in Winnipeg, and it seems completely self-evident that no one round here has the faintest idea what Attila the Stockbroker is. The gig has been organised at very short notice by the Winnipeg Folk Festival; as far as I can tell, the publicity consists of a box ad in the hotel restaurant menu and a couple of leaflets shoved between the Grateful Dead albums in the local second-hand record store. There is a two-dollar admission charge, waived for anyone staying at or entertaining in the hotel.

The majority of the audience consists of businessmen; corporate males, each with one of those little cardboard identification badges which middle-aged executives wear in lieu of personalities when they go to business functions in hotels. They are all rather drunk, and obviously under the impression that Attila the Stockbroker is some kind of country and western act.

There's a smattering of Folk Club regulars, mostly Woodstock survivors and Aran sweater victims, and, to my pleasure and surprise, a group of ten or so who look like punks and show every sign of interest – in fact virtually all of them come up to me individually during the course of the evening and ask me why the hell I'm playing at a country and western club instead of the local anarcho-veggie commune, and will I come and play for them there after I've been booed off?

At the appointed hour I take the stage. Directly in front of me, and seemingly oblivious of my presence, four gentlemen of the wrist talk corporate gunk – their lapel badges indicating an umbilical allegiance to a local computer firm. Summoning up all my considerable energy reserves, I launch into an extra loud, extra fast version of 'Libyan Students From Hell' and await the onslaught.

An hour and a half and three encores later, I leave the stage – very worried.

Australia

I'm not much one for snapshots, though the world is now my oyster
I chronicle my wanderings in poem and in song
But when I went Down Under, I brought along my camera
to photograph the wildlife, that rich and teeming throng
On my first few days in Oz, I wasn't sure that they existed –
those strange, exotic species, they mostly hide away
But on the way to Melbourne the truth became apparent;
if you want to see some wildlife, then take the motorway...

There are wallabies and wombats, there are possums, birds and lizards
and kangaroos of all sorts, yes, even a big red
and all these different species have one quality in common
yes, each of them is wonderfully, spectacularly dead...

There are lots of flies in Oz, and now I know where they all come
        from
for there were lots of maggots in the creatures that I saw
yes, every little corpsie was a blowfly kindergarten –
more wrigglers and more squirmers than I've ever seen before
Now I've made my contribution to Australian natural history
and it's by way of a tribute that I decomposed this song
but one word of advice to all you wild death photographers:
stay inside the car because the bastards don't half pong!

And with a squelch, another hapless kanga rues the day
that the Government of Victoria built that new Hume Motorway...

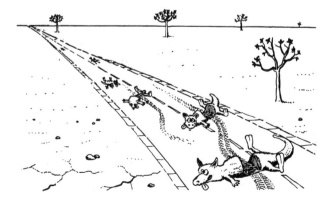

Xenophobia

(a satirical look at the English attitude to Europe – strange how the xenophobic attitude of 'our' football thugs is mirrored, albeit in a slightly more subtle way, by the Conservative Government, and in a slightly less subtle way (!) by the tabloids)

THE DUTCH the Dutch they're much too much we're gonna kick them in the crutch flick bogies at the slimy wogs and trip them up with their own clogs we'll twist their ears and break their glasses stick their tulips up their arses foul their windmills with our bowels and vomit into their canals THE DANES the Danes we'll bash their brains and wire their willies to the mains boycott their bacon and their prawns and go and piss over their lawns the scabby Scandinavian scum got scrotal scabies of the bum they live on fish heads and weak tea their lager tastes like canine pee THE SWISS the Swiss they stink of piss no race more tedious than this with cuckoo clocks and huge amounts of money in their bank accounts they may be rich but we don't care we'll shave off all their pubic hair and make them live in Belgium – that's the right place for the boring prats THE FRENCH the French they smell like tench we'll chase them all into a trench get loads of garlic on our breath and suffocate them all to death we don't like onions snails or Proust so smeg off Frogs we rule the roost you may be existentialists but we're dead hard and we get pissed THE CZECHS the Czechs they're scared of sex they've all got crabs and skinny necks their cars are shit their beer's too strong we're not gonna stay there for long there's absolutely zilch to do there's no Black Label and no glue so we'll just wreck the place and go and leave them to their queues and snow THE FINNS the Finns live out of tins they all look like the Cocteau Twins their scenery's not very nice 'cos most of it's a mass of ice so don't go there it's much too chilly you'll end up with a frozen willy it's a godforsaken hole obscenely close to the north pole THE KRAUTS the Krauts they think they're louts but I've seen nastier Brussels sprouts they strut around like football yobs but they're all talk and cheesy knobs they live on pickled vegetation what a fucking stupid nation all their nipples are bright green the strangest folk I've ever seen THE SWEDES the Swedes well they're all weeds and all their cities look like Leeds they walk around with plastic bags and noses stuck in porno mags they live on fish just like the Danes but they've got even smaller brains their language sounds like double dutch their land smells like a llama's crutch THE GREEKS the Greeks those fucking geeks we'll lock 'em up in bogs for weeks puke in their restaurants and bars and write rude slogans on their cars we'll get a load of herpes scabs and stick 'em all in their kebabs and write a note – in puke – to say 'CLUB 18-30 RULE OK! THE POLES the Poles eat toilet rolls their underpants are full of holes they have to queue over an hour to get a mouldy cauliflower they whine and whinge and gripe and moan and play the hairy pink trombone they're always wanking in the loo there's fuck all else for them to do THE YANKS the Yanks......der, many thanks for giving us your bombs and tanks protecting us from Arab hordes and bringing herpes and skateboards you're foreigners but you're alright 'cos you speak English and you fight or so it tells me in *The Sun* ...Oi! Being a moron is such fun!

41

Four Song Lyrics

1. *The Pen and the Sword*
(for Salman Rushdie)

You never thought that it would come to this
they took your freedom
now they want your life
Here's to you in your distress
Poet on the run to a safe address
Man of words in the shadow of the knife

You told of life in an inhospitable land
of a satirist
and a city made of sand
You wrote it for your brothers
and they burned it in the street
and the Union Jack said 'send them back'
...to make the irony complete

A refugee from another century
where the world is absolute
and words queue up to die
Where the page is a flame
and the truth has a single name
Where womanhood is crushed to the sound of an anguished cry

They say the pen is mightier than the sword
The poet will never call the tyrant lord
But when the sword is raised what can you do
when all you've got is a pen
and they're coming after you...?

When they were brownshirts
they were soon abused
But a new disguise leaves some people confused
But if we won't stand up and be counted –
well, it happened once before
Remember Pastor Niemöller
as you hide behind the door

A refugee from another century
where the world is absolute
and words queue up to die
Where the page is a flame
and the truth has a single name
Where womanhood is crushed to the sound of an anguished cry
to the sound of an anguished cry
in the name of an ancient lie...

You never thought that it would come to this
they took your freedom
now they want your life
Here's to you in your distress
Poet on the run to a safe address
Man of words in the shadow of the knife

2. *This Is Free Europe*

Dead of night in Carpentras
brings the ghosts from the days of Vichy
Broken windows in the high street
Swastikas in the cemetery
Blond young men on a Rostock evening
Beer and loathing on their breath
Ten to one like their cowardly fathers
Arms outstretched in the sign of death

CHORUS

If it takes a voice then shout the truth
If it takes a hand then hold them back
If it takes a fist then strike them down
From Cable Street to Hoyerswerda
Pamyat, Schönhuber and Le Pen –
THIS IS FREE EUROPE...NEVER AGAIN!

Afternoon in a Soviet city
Now they don't even need to hide
Blue shirted thugs advertise their pogroms
None are arrested, none are tried
'Pamyat' means 'a memory' –
What memories for these Russian Nazis?
Children killed in front of their mothers
Human skin turned into lampshades

CHORUS

Once more we see the darkness in the European soul
As the chains fall there comes an awful beast
His eyes are staring, and there is hell upon his brow –
Oscar, François, Gregor, Tanya listen to me now...

I'm a Jew in Carpentras
I'm a Jew in that Soviet city
I'm an Asian in the East End
I'm a Cuban in East Germany
Don't tell me it doesn't concern us
It's not something to ignore
They are feeding on our apathy –
That's how it began before...

CHORUS

This is for Jörg Wolter and all my friends in East Germany

3. Market Sector One (Summer 1990)

Another new year and too much beer and goodbye to the Wall
But now there's only disappointment, nothing left at all
The dreams we marched and fought for have faded and turned sour
The cabbage is a king now,* it's Helmut's finest hour
and on the streets the people want it 'as seen on TV'
and a big bunch of bananas is a sign that you are free
It's just begun –
Market Sector One

As in the East they talk about a future bold and new
a thousand Western businessmen are celebrating too
The vultures are all circling 'cos there's money to be made
a multinational carve-up, a bank to be obeyed
And now the old, rich foreigners make claims on every hand
'You're living in my house, mein Herr, you're farming on my land'
It's time to run –
Market Sector One

Is that all that we were fighting for?
Landlords and sex shops, nothing more?
Welcome to the Western dream
Welcome to the cheap labour scheme

The whole of Europe's changing – Big Brother's on the run
It could just be a brand new age of freedom has begun
But freedom doesn't bow its head to some financier's will
And Europe is our common home – not some gigantic till
So send the moneygrabbers riding off into the sun
And take your assets in your own hands, answerable to none
Then we'll have fun
And justice will be done...

* 'Kohl' is German for 'cabbage'

45

4. *Tyler Smiles*
(22nd November 1990)

Here's to you, the sceptic few
in the dark old days of '82
when a thousand corpses stoked an awful pyre
Here's to '84 and '5
when all our dreams took another dive
midst the jeers of Mammon and the howls of the Digger's choir
There were times I really thought
they'd all been conned and all been bought
Too much Chingford on the brain
and never going to think again
But it's a taxing time for Essex now...

And Tyler smiles, Tyler smiles
on an angry crowd stretching miles and miles
Six hundred years but the lesson wasn't learned
And Tyler smiles, Tyler smiles
through a hail of bricks and stones and tiles
Now history rolls back,
the worm has turned,
retribution earned.

Tell me why it took so long
all these years we've sung this song
and will the spectre ever go away?
A hundred thousand garden gnomes
outside a hundred thousand homes
are standing on their own two feet' today
No strident tones now, just a whine
a hand-picked bank clerk holds the line
The same song with a few new chords
for Albion's user-friendly hordes
A thornless rose is bending in the breeze

And Tyler smiles, Tyler smiles
through the acid rain and the sheepdog trials
Perhaps he never really went away
And Tyler smiles, Tyler smiles
on the village greens and the seven dials –
there's still a bit of fight in us today!
Tyler smiles.

46

And if it's really over, and the swords turn into ploughshares
She'll go to Eastern Europe, oh they really love her there
The fool Walesa and the iron curse

And Tyler smiles, Tyler smiles
as Labour's leaders close their files
on 'Wat's his name' from their own history

And Tyler smiles, Tyler smiles
on that angry crowd stretching miles and miles –
'Hey – Gotcha, lady! Gotcha, finally…'
Tyler smiles.

Written a few days after the fall of Margaret Thatcher

Rain

Rain
is grass.
The flooded lake
is a summer meadow.
So you, my darling,
being seven-tenths water,
are a cricket pitch.
And I am the heavy roller
in the morning dew.

Did YOU buy a used British Gas share from this government?

Tell Sid

he's a nonexistent totally fictitious dork created at a ridiculous cost to us taxpayers by the spectacularly unimaginative alcohol-sodden Mogadon-brained gnomes of some tinpot advertising agency in order to persuade thousands of upwardly mobile and extremely acquisitive I'm-alright-Jack council-house-owning stone-cladding garden-gnome and MFI furniture-worshipping downmarket cutprice would-be J. Paul Gettys to open their poxy little piggy banks and invest their hard-earned pennies in a public amenity which until very recently belonged to them anyway! TELL SID that it's not travellers who waste taxpayers' money as his amoeba-brained drinking mates seem to think but corrupt slimy government officials who sell off our industries at knockdown prices to their corporate friends and puke-inducing scum in suits handed vastly profitable public monopolies on a plate who then pay themselves vast salaries while sacking half their workforce! TELL SID that the only reason the government wanted insignificant little nobodies like him to indulge his pathetic Howard Hughes fantasies and grab a pitifully irrelevant handful of meaningless shares in the first place was so that they it could send him a threatening letter come election time telling him that should he have the effrontery to vote for the evil Libyan-sponsored Saddam Hussein-fellating child molesters of the Labour Party his tiny little pound of flesh would go up in smoke and that therefore out of sheer naked nude bare unadorned self-interest he should vote Conservative! And if dear old non-existent SID is so mind-bogglingly, groin-tremblingly THICK that he still can't understand what the bastards are trying to do then just TELL SID that *The Sun* Says That British Gas Shares Give You Aids And Turn You Into A Lesbian And Gay!

Dedicated to the considerable number of rappers who are for-
ever boasting inanely about their guns and their penises, talking
about women in appallingly degrading terms, advocating violence
against homosexuals, allying themselves with anti-Semitic crypto-
fascists. If they were white, their misogynistic, homophobic, reac-
tionary nonsense would be treated with the contempt it deserves.
Because they're black, loads of guilt-ridden white middle-class
journalists – especially music journalists – fawn over them. This
is exceptionally stupid and should stop RIGHT NOW.

The Iron Men of Rap

You're the iron men rappers with your big gold chains
You talk like the clappers but you don't use your brains
The Grandmaster's Message made me hold my breath
but now I'd rather listen to Lawnmower Deth!
You rap about your GOLD and you rap about your CAR
and you rap about what good rappers you are
you rap about your GUNS and the money you make
and the size of your ONE-EYED TROUSER SNAKE
You say it's bigger than the Albert Hall
but I bet it's like an earthworm, very very small
You say it's bigger than the Albert Hall
but I bet it's like a maggot or you ain't got one at all!
You run on stage with your guns in a rage
like angry prisoners fresh out of the cage
Your finger's on the trigger and you wanna ENGAGE
turning on the chill in the new Ice Age
And there's violence, violence in the air
but some of you like it, you don't seem to care
And there's violence, violence in the air
but some of you like it, you don't seem to care
Now I don't like the DOLLAR and I don't like the GUN
and the (w)rapping they come in don't bother me none
I wanna rap fast and I wanna have fun
And I mean HAVE FUN not shoot someone!

With your massive testicles and concrete cock
Gonna bust a gonad every time you rock!
Every move in your body is designed to shock
So yo! there shepherd boy, how's your flock?
Now I don't wanna hear about segregation
Don't wanna hear about your perfect nation
Don't wanna hear about Farrakhan
Cos Farrakhan is an evil man
And hey everybody, let's make a show
Cos if Farrakhan gets you, you're gonna go!
From the hair on my head to my hairy scro'
I'm out of the bottle and I'm ready to blow...

The rap I rap is black and white
This rap says unionise, don't fight
This rap doesn't wallow in liberal guilt
It just says equal up to the hilt
This rap's got a penis of average size
Not a huge great whale flopping out of its flies
No gold, no chains, no hype, no lies
Just a thinking brain and a pair of sharp eyes
So wise up, rappers – and before you spout
Find something original to rap about!
I've had my say, now it's over and out
From MC Attila the poetry tout
Said MC Attila – signing out!

But, of course, not all rappers conform to this crude stereotype!
MC Trainspotter, the world's first rapping trainspotter, certainly
doesn't...He knows you don't have to be really tough and live
somewhere dangerous and have a gun and a big penis to be a
rapper!

Boys in the Hood
(Trainspotter Rap)

MC Trainspotter, yeah, that's me
– and this is my homeboy,
Nice-T!
Now some people think that trainspotting's rot...
but me and my posse, we say
IT'S NOT!
All you need is a camera, notebook and pen
you write down a number, then you write one down again
We're ignored by the nation, we go down the station
and we've got another hobby –
masturbation
Hey, don't walk away, 'cos I'm talking to you
You know what they call us –
The Platform 2 Live Crew!
Now me & my homeboys work in a bank
and at the weekend
we go to the library
On Saturday mornings we like shopping
and then we go
amateur league groundhopping
I nearly caught pneumonia at Billingham Synthonia
Wanna know the layout of the ground?
I'll phone ya!
And at half time I've got everything I need
A nice telephone directory
to read
MC Trainspotter in the house
I've got the suss, and I've got the nous
I don't live in a ghetto like those rappers in the States
I like the police
Yes, they're my best mates...

I've never been arrested
(that goes without saying)
I've reported lots of people I've seen
travelling without paying
And here's what I say to every other rapping crew –
well, I'm OK at rapping
but I'm not as good as you!
But I do think
you spend far too much on your gear
I could save you some money
so please listen here:
My trainers are from Oxfam and they cost 50p
My anorak's my mum's and the carrier bag was free!
I wouldn't like a gold chain – somebody might mug me
and I don't want a baseball cap – they really bug me!
We're the parka posse, we're the 'boys in the hood'
and it keeps out the rain – now isn't that good?
And if you want information
down at the station
just ask me, it'll fill me with elation!
MC Trainspotter – yeah, that's me
Yo! there, homeboy!
Want a cup of tea?

For Clive Ponting, Sarah Tisdall, and all those who follow in their footsteps...

Rapping Mole

I'm Rapping Mole from Leaky Hole, who I am you'll never guess –
Got a secret code on an angry road to an underground address
I'm a real cool cat with a photostat of a secret document
And when I leak it brings a shriek from the deadhead government!

Cos I'm Rapping Mole from Leaky Hole and I'm driving the
          politicians up the pole
Belgrano or the missile bases, Ministers all get red faces
At my desk behind the scenes, I bin the lies and spill the beans
With a rap rap rap I cut the crap and tell my tales to magazines!

Kim Philby was my hero – he showed me how it's done
And Tony Blunt's a clever bloke – he really had some fun
Us funky moles get everywhere – this cat can surely rock it
And I've got my funky blackmail cheque right here in my back
          pocket
My eyes are sharp, my member huge – I'm the hip-hop priest of
          subterfuge
This mole's got soul, he knows his role – this mole's got style, he
          makes you smile
The Sieve-all Service is named well – it's like a sieve, it leaks like
          hell
so bang bang bang come join the gang, let's freak and leak and do
          our thang!

Don't worry Mr Minister – don't moan and make a fuss
Just leave your file with a happy smile – your secret's safe with us
Oh, naughty Mr Minister – this cover-up won't do!
Your wife, mistress and hamster would all be ashamed of you
So while you sleep I creep, creep, creep to a photostat machine
and soon your lies are on their way to a left-wing magazine
and then the feline is among the pigeons, that's for sure –
your secret's out, so scream and shout, you bottom-faced old bore...

'Cos I'm Rapping Mole from Leaky Hole and I'm driving the
      politicians up the pole
Got a secret code on an angry road – gonna spill the beans and
      shoot my load!
I'm a real cool cat with a photostat – I'm a fruit bat wombat acrobat!
And when I leak the pinstripes freak so watch out, geek, your
      future's bleak!

Said 1, 2, 1, 2, 3 – spying for the CND!
4, 5, 4, 5, 6 – we know all of Whitehall's tricks!
7, 8, 7, 8, 9 – spill the beans and watch 'em whine!
9, 10, 9, 10, 11 – all good rappers go to heaven!

Got soul, little doll, I know my role, I'm top of the poll –
I'm RAPPING MOLE!

This piece chronicles one of the high spots in the history of my favourite football club Brighton's rivalry with Crystal Palace – with absolutely no apologies to Paul Hardcastle's appalling 1980s disco hit 'N-n-n-nineteen'...

Tuesday September 12 1989 began like any other day in the footballing calendar, with newly-discovered Team of the 80s, Crystal Palace, travelling to Anfield to test their Colditz-like defensive qualities and mesmerising attacking skills against the sacrificial lemmings of Liverpool. Now football is a funny game, as the utterly retarded cliché goes, and on this particular evening it proved to be a very funny game indeed, in fact a positively hilarious and sidesplittingly humourous one, even more mirth-inducing than Princess Diana trying to define existentialism or William Waldegrave having sex with a paper-shredding machine. For while Palace's much-feared rivals Brighton & Hove Albion were slaughtering Wolverhampton Wanderers 4-2, at Anfield the final score was Liverpool 9, Crystal Palace 0. Liverpool 9, Crystal Palace nil. N-n-n-nine nil, nine nil. N-n-n-nine nil, nine nil. And following those fateful n-n-n-ninety minutes on that hilarious Tuesday night the hapless halibuts from Selhurst Park were subjected to fierce and merciless ridicule from the rest of the football world and many of them are still living out their experiences to this day. Even now the South London branch of the Samaritans are receiving streams of mysterious phone calls where the only audible sounds are donkey-like voices braying bewilderedly 'Nine-nil. N-n-n-nine nil. Ee-aw! Nine nil. N-n-n-nine nil. Ee-aw!' And when the Palace players got home, obviously in need of moral support and counselling following their torrid n-n-n-nine nil experience, none of them received a hero's welcome. None of them. None of them received a hero's welcome. N-n-n-none of them. The long-term effects of such an unbelievable n-n-n-nine nil stonking are hard to predict, but it seems likely that many of the Crystal Palace squad may be so demoralised that they may be forced to leave professional football and sign on. S-s-s-sign on. Sign on. S-s-s-sign on. S-s-s-sign on, sign on. S-s-s-sign on, sign on. A worse fate even than this may well befall the Palace goalkeeper Perry Suckling, a man who, rather like the Queen Mother, wears gloves for no apparent reason, for his intense feelings of humiliation may well lead him to sign on in Vietnam. V-v-v-Vietnam. S-s-s-sign on. V-v-v-Vietnam. S-s-s-sign on. V-v-v-Vietnam. S-s-s-sign on (repeat ad nauseam)

...And Smith Must Score!

Five yards out, an open goal
and not a man in sight...
The memory of that awful miss
still haunts me late at night
Ten seconds left in extra time
and history in the making
but Smith's shot hit the goalie's legs
and now our hearts are breaking

A paraplegic lemming
with the skill of a dead cat
and the finesse of a hamster
could have done better than that!
A decomposing dogfish
wrapped in bondage, head to toe
could have stuck that ball into the net
but Gordon Smith? Oh, no!

When Robinson broke down the left
and put the ball across
we knew for sure the Seagulls' win
was Man United's loss
And as old Smithy shaped to shoot
a mighty roar went up –
The impossible had happened!
WE'D WON THE F.A.CUP!

A fleeting glimpse of glory:
alas, 'twas not to be...
We lost the replay 4–0
now we're in Division Three
The one chance of a lifetime
so cruelly snatched away
But till the white coats come for me
I'll ne'er forget that day...

Dustbin Poem

Today I took out the rubbish
and thought of you.
At the bottom of my dustbin
the maggots wriggled round and round
like planes circling over Heathrow Airport.
Now and then
two larval aviators collided
in the crowded, circular, putrescent grooves of metal
and I thought yes, this is us –
not even ships that pass in the night
but maggots wriggling in predetermined circles
in the putrescent dustbin
of the enterprise culture.

Video Nazis

i.e. – the new breed of sadistic crypto-fascists who enjoy making
or watching films depicting other human beings being tortured
and destroyed in a variety of hideous ways (and don't tell me
it's only a movie...)

In Rome the gladiators fought
while people slobbered in the stands
The bloodlust rose, the voyeurs wanked
with transfixed gaze and frenzied hands
Then naked humans thrown to beasts
were torn apart amidst the cheers
Their last entreaties drowned in blood
and wine-soaked sick sadistic jeers

And still it swells, the evil lust
centuries old and still unslaked
The cesspit of the human mind
The vampire free, unchained, unstaked
And now sick men – it's always men –
are harnessing the stinking vulture
lurking in the human soul
and flaunting it as video culture

Film-makers, impotent and scared
with shrivelled pricks and sick desires
hate women so they burn their breasts
or wrench their nipples off with pliers
And hipsters in the glossy press
say 'What's the fuss? It's special effects.'
It's real enough in those bastards' minds –
I want to break their fucking necks!

And what of those who watch the films
of Nazis raping Jewish mothers?
Do they sit there, and wank, and spout
wish they'd been there beside the others
then play with children of their own
like S.S. butchers used to do?
Look in the mirror, nasty man –
see Adolf Eichmann stare at you!

In 1982, after Lord Denning had ruled Ken Livingstone's GLC fares policy illegal, forcing massive increases in London Transport fares, I wrote a piece called 'Awayday' about the perils of a day out in London with the Law Lords. In the light of (Ex Comrade) Yeltsin's activities in Russia I thought it was time for an update – so here we go on the perils of a day's shopping in the new, 'democratic' 'CIS' (which I always thought meant Co-operative Insurance Society, actually)

woke up got up read the post attacked the postman took the rat for a walk but hordes of starving children grabbed it and ate it raw came back fed the amoeba but it still wasn't big enough to be seen with the naked eye so i thought i'd fatten it up a bit more before i put it in the casserole emptied the flower pot and made some coffee invented a new machine which produces genuine 100% beef hamburgers out of old copies of lenin's memoirs while simultaneously reconciling the armenians and azerbajanis wrote a passionate love letter to the head of cis food distribution who happens to be a small crucian carp then thought i'm bored think i'll go to moscow cos moscow's got to be more interesting than the eec catering size frankfurter tin i've lived in since my house was repossessed by the original pre-revolutionary owners and i might be able to pick up some bucks fizz bootlegs or the latest jean-paul sartre dub lp got the bus two hours late got the train four hours late train was delayed for a week due to huge crowds of pimps drug dealers americans gangsters child pornographers and manic street preachers fans celebrating the restoration of capitalism and the collapse of soviet power got to moscow went into the bread shop queued for nine hours loaf of bread please sure mate that'll be a hundred roubles what d'you mean a hundred roubles it was only ten kopeks last week i'm not paying a hundred roubles for a loaf of bread sorry mate i know it was only ten kopeks last week but an unstable semi-alcoholic egomaniac authoritarian opportunist who spent forty odd years as an unquestioning stalinist apparatchik slavishly toeing the party line had a few words with margaret thatcher and then reconstituted himself as a paragon of freedom has taken power and turned the country into a devil take the hindmost and sod you mate milton friedman obsessed dump where everything that moves is privatised and the prices have gone up ten thousand per cent that'll be a hundred roubles please…bollocks to that i said and after a short pregnant pause all the people behind me in the queue plucked up courage and said bollocks to that and all the homeless starving people begging in the streets said bollocks to that and all the jews victimised by openly marauding anti-semitic gangs encouraged by the authorities said bollocks to that and all the war veterans who defended leningrad not st petersburg said bollocks to that and the relatives of all the people killed in the interethnic wars said bollocks to that and the mothers of all the kids murdered by gangsters and ravaged by drugs and left to die for want of hospital treatment said bollocks to that and the millions of people thrown on the scrapheap all over eastern europe in the name of rationalisation and profitability and market forces said bollocks to that and the relatives of the victims of the nationalistic orgies in yugoslavia and the pogroms in east germany and the hopeless hunger in albania said bollocks to that and all the brave, hopeful, creative people totally unimpressed by the painted McDonalds smile and the crisp IMF banknote and the leer of the advertising hoarding and the soulless chatter of the world money market and the brainless yelling of the tabloid and the obscene illusion of 'freedom' in a starving, violence-racked, fascist-infested continent said bollocks to that and we're forming a mass revolutionary party with a brand new vision and we're going to wave the red flag again and we're going to take power again and next time we're not going to confuse perestroika with selling out to capitalism and our slogan manifesto and progreamme is going to be bread peace and land...and...bollocks to that...!

[June 1992]

61

63